PERCEPTIONS OF THE MIND

(The Truth Within Us)

By John Fine

March 12, 2011

"Dedicated to the Human Race"

Edited by Janet L. Fine

1

ISBN 978-1-105-48467-4

2

Perceptions of the Mind

Contents

The "Why" behind This Book

About the Author

of my journey, I had figured out that "God" had a different

plan and route for me to take. In its completion, I was able

to realize the very nature of "God" and man with the

responsibility of all to the known universe. It is my hope

that all my readers can share in this journey I went through,

and in the end, they too will come to know the same

conclusions as I did once their journey is over. This

journey is, however, a mere step into the unknown future

and only time will determine the next step of either a very

long story or a very short story. This choice is ours to

make and will be determined by how we act for future

generations.

About the Author

I was raised by a strict, authoritarian type father who believed in the ethics of hard work, God and Country. We were judged by the fruits of our labor and a man was only as good as his word. I lived in mostly rural America and stayed mostly within the central states until manhood, where most of my time was spent in southern Georgia. I was able, while employed by the United States Army, to acquire many different skills and was able to explore many areas of culture and social entities that most likely would not have been explored if I had not decided to enter into the service. I have belonged to countless numbers of churches, cults, gangs, and organizations over the years. I have lived all over the world and within many places of the United

States. I have had many hardships to include death, fire, burglary, and many types of abuse, drowning, homelessness, hunger, divorce and much more. I have interacted with the richest of folks and slept on the streets with the poorest of folks. I have had jobs of many shapes and sizes, and now I am the proud father of six children. I have always considered myself to be a good old country boy who loves all life and takes pleasure in being able to give pleasure to those around me. When I help a person crack a smile and feel well about themselves, it is a joy just to witness that emotion within their mind set. I have been called a perfectionist but disagree and call myself an analytical enthusiast instead. Through all my joys and pains, I have always tried to keep a level head and explore things within the boundaries that we have created for ourselves. This book, I believe, was inspired by forces unknown, the collective experiences of my life, the collective experiences, beliefs, and writings of others, and recorded history. I have taken my analytical skills as a technician and applied them to the human race. I have only one hope behind this book, that it helps me build, with others, a future my kids can hold dear to themselves and a future that is sustainable with sustainable methods for generations to come.

Perceptions of the Mind

Chapter I

The Genesis

As the human mind progresses through life experiences, our perceptions change from one experience to the next. We are given an environmental approach to those experiences then it is transformed into a social grouping which initiates our actions towards ourselves and humanity. In this book, I will make an attempt of explaining, the perceptions of the mind in an analytical process, that is totally free of prejudice, bias and social stimulations. Research has found that perception of the mind begins after a child is born from the mother's womb. (Piaget, 1972) These perceptions are entered into the brain and begin our environmental development. As we get older, this development is influenced by not only our environment, but believed by many theorists, several other areas of influence as well. (Human Development, 2011) After reading many reports, books, and documents put out by leading people in the area of human development; I then had to sum up what I read in one word; I would say that one word would be "Environment". All these people seem to agree, in one way or the other, that our environment places the largest role in one's development of their perceptions.

Now, since our environment is the best source of our cognitive perception; then how do we obtain knowledge of that perception? Well, this knowledge is obtained by the five senses, (Sight, Touch, Hear, Smell, and Taste) (A. Zamora, 2006) Once this knowledge is obtained, we

travel through a journey in the mind that takes us
through many stages and these stages are called "States
of Mind" (Ian Heath, 2003) These states of mind are
basically the mind set we are in at that point of our life
as our knowledge grows, our perceptions grow and our
state of mind grows (or changes) as well. How do we
allow growth of this knowledge, perceptions, and state
of mind? Well, we take our five senses and we
assimilate everything with which we come in contact.

Assimilation of knowledge (learned acquisitions) can
be in the positive and negative realm. The information
we receive can come from many sources such as
parents, books, schools, personal contact, history, media
and many other areas of contact. (S. Canney, 2011)
Now let's take a look at the positive assimilation on an
individual level. Positive assimilation is where the
knowledge or information we receive has an outcome
that affects our environment and us in a positive way

with the finalization of positive results. For instance, a person goes to college to learn about heart disease, gets his or hers PHD in that field, then later on in their life develops the cure for heart disease. This would be considered a positive assimilation with a positive outcome. Negative assimilation is where the knowledge or information we receive has an outcome that affects our environment and us in a negative way with the finalization of negative results. For instance, a person hears that "crystal meth" gives an unforgettable high so they try the drug and the drug, which is nothing more than toxic waste, enters the body and makes its way to the heart and brain, shutting down both systems until the life in the person is no more. This would be considered negative assimilation with a negative result. Both positive and negative assimilation can interact with one another, each causing much different results. For instance, a child touches a stove that is hot and gets burned; and then the next time the child is in front of

the stove they choose not to touch it because they know

it will burn them. This is where a negative assimilation

turns into a positive one.   On the other hand, say a

child is taught all the effects of alcohol and how it will

impair their judgment if it's abused; which in turn can

cause a negative effect. The child does not believe this

information and decides to get drunk with their buddies

then they all drive from the bar. Because of their

impaired judgment, they are driving in speeds that the

automobile is incapable of maintaining on the current

terrain. So it is impelled one hundred feet into the air,

levels the tree tops, then is mangled beyond recognition

and all of the occupants of the vehicle are ripped to

pieces and their lives are no more. This would be where

positive assimilation turns into a negative one. Both

positive and negative assimilation are important for us

to maintain a healthy interaction with ourselves and

other humans. But with our focus on the positive,

studies have shown this to have better results than the

negative although we need both for our survival.

(LiveStrong.com, 2011)

On a Global level the positive and negative effects on

humans can have similar effects on our planet and

environment, but the negative effects, on the before

mentioned areas, can become irreversible over time.

Like us (humans), the earth is a living organism

(Unexplainable. Net 2011) and can be affected by

perceptions of the mind. So what I have learned

through life and through research is that as long as we

focus on the positive assimilation of all that affects the

human or the human race and act on that, then the

balance between positive and negative remain in

harmony with each other. However, if we shift our

focus to the negative then this will result in an

imbalance which leads to some form of destruction. I

will now give two examples of this in five key social arenas which are politics, economics, religion, culture, and entertainment.

Politics: On the positive side, a person goes to college, learns about the political field, goes on to become a senator then writes a bill that abolishes violent sex offenders from living in or around schools and thousands of children are protected as the result. *This is a very positive outcome and a great example where negative and positive is in harmony or balanced.* On the negative side, this same person goes to college, learns about politics, works his way up through the ranks of politics then becomes the leader of his country. He uses that leadership to fuel his personal hatred towards a certain group of people and destroys thousands of lives during his reign of terror. *This is a very negative outcome and a great example where negative and positive are not in harmony.*

Religion: On the positive side a person or group learns about starvation in Africa then use all their current available resources to aid as many people as they can. On the negative side, a disease has infected thousands and they believe it to be the work of the devil so they destroy thousands of infected people before they can infect others, and cut out the tongue of those who speak up and say it's just a disease and can be treated medically. *These are both great examples of the positive and negative sides but both to this day remain out of harmony due to disqualifying factors.* As with these and others, the game is the same just different players, and the outcome is the same, as well. Our understanding of the circumstance can change the outcome but only once we have reached that level of understanding. History records time and time again where mankind's

18

ignorance caused the death of thousands in all the

above arenas and the only time it changed was when

our understanding and perception allowed change to

happen. One thing that is certain is that this change of

our perception did not take place until we were able to

admit that our previous perception was wrong and

needed to be changed. For instance, when we thought

the world was flat, after one man dared to embark on a

journey beyond the edge of the world, we than realized

that the world was in fact round.

Chapter II

The Realization

Once we realize we need or have to change, our world becomes new and we begin to see things from a different perspective. It is this perspective that launches us to either status quo or to our next level of perception. In my own life, I have had many perceptions and on many levels. I have experienced life in ways that most only read about in books. I have interacted with every level of the social, culture, and religious ladder. I have eaten the finest meals as well as dug through garbage cans for my next meal. I have slept in the finest hotels and on the streets. I have belonged to countless religious and cult organizations, lived in over ten different states, visited over twenty different states, lived in four different countries, and visited numerous others. I have had long hair, spiked hair with ear rings, and no hair. I have partied with the rich as well as the poor, drank the finest of coffees with fine china as well as coffee that was made on a camp fire in a rusty can. I have watched Disney on Ice and then children playing with a rattle snake. I have had brushed with death on many different occasions and have buried many of my own. I have known many people from all walks of life and from many parts of the world and have interacted with many different social mediums throughout my life. I am a technician by trade but have worked as a ranch hand, dishwasher, busboy, janitor, custodian, cook, waiter, stock boy, cashier, assistant manager, army soldier, painter, teacher, instructor, and owned my own business. So to say that through life experiences I am a well rounded person; would be an understatement.

The one thing that has remained constant throughout my life is that the moment of realization where my perception changed, I was overcome by a sudden burst of euphoria which was followed by a feeling of emptiness that became filled with the excitement of the new perception. Each time this happened in my life I felt as if I became stronger in knowledge and wiser in the world. This euphoria has been described as an out of body experience, a religious experience, and a coming into focus experience. After much study, I have found that this feeling was a *biological, physiological or emotional* change that happens when someone metamorphoses because of their perception. (R. Firehammer, 2004)

Recently I underwent several metamorphoses because of a perception I encountered. I was asked three simple questions and because of those questions my perception of how things were and how they are now were forever changed. The first question was asked by a former student of mine, who one could say was in the upper percentile of knowledge and how to use that knowledge. This student was one of the elite students in the school I was teaching in and I have always believed him to have a level of intelligence superior to most. He also had a level of common sense that was equally superior. One day we were discussing a topic and during our discussion he asked me a simple question. At first, I responded with the usual non-supportable statements that most people use when they have nothing intelligent to add to the conversation. Then I decided I was going to prove to this student, through research, that he was wrong with his beliefs and I knew for sure that I was going to prove this without a shadow of doubt. The question was "Did God

23

create man in his image or did man create God in his image"? Well, this should have been an easy question to answer; but as I started to do my research on this subject, I was approached by another person around this same time frame who asked me another question. Through that question I discovered yet another question to be answered. Little did I know that these three questions would change my perception to the point where a metamorphosis took place causing a new perception of the mind that I am only starting to realize the impact and complexity of its implications. The question that was asked was, "Did I know what Zeitgeist was"? In researching that question, I discovered a question of my own which was "What was the Venus Project"?

In exploring these questions, I found the answer I needed for the first question asked while exploring the other two. My answers that were discovered or uncovered were not of my liking and rational thought would not allow me to simply dismiss this information because it was recorded truth. What were these truths? Well, at that moment I thought that the very beliefs that Christians and other religions around the world hold dear and true are nothing more than "Plagiarism" from religions of ancient times. (Ancient Religions, 2011) This plagiarism was re-packaged into more acceptable packages called the Bible, the Avesta, the Quran, the Hadith, the writings of Bahaullah and the list goes on and on (World Religions, 2011). All these documents have been made to appear authentic then widely dispersed to nations around the world. I was a very big believer in the Bible mainly because I believed the information within its pages was authentic and written by men who were inspired by God. The problem with this, is most of what is written and practiced in the Bible was written and practiced in ancient religions centuries

25

before Moses, Jesus, and his disciples were ever born, (E. Carpenter, 2011) (Online Reader, 2011) the references listed were only a few of many that I found as I did my research. When I referenced ancient symbols I was shock to find that many of the ancient religions used the very symbols that many believers of different faiths use today and believe that these symbols were born of their faith, when in fact they were first used centuries before their faith or their previous believer's were ever born. For example, the "Christian born" symbols of the "cross" and the "fish" were used by the Egyptians, Pagans (seiyaku.com) and is referenced in the signs of the Zodiac used in days of old. (Pagan and Christian Creed, 2011) Not to mention that the dates, holidays, and traditions that were used in ancient times are the same dates, holidays, and traditions used today with religions around the world, just not as primitive as they once were. So you can see by this time my perceptions were on a dismal spiral roll and were

about to become even more adventurous.

Chapter III

The Future

My future had always been set, I had always believed that I would live my life and watch man destroy all the things we hold dear then one day everything would be destroyed and I would be sent to Heaven. Now in the light of my new perceptions, I was not sure that this was the path for me. With these new perceptions I started to see a pattern of a universal psychosis that humans shared across the planet. This psychosis was in the areas of the "Doomsday" theory, governmental entities, and religious entities. I once read in a book a quote from Albert Einstein (Einstein Quotes, 2011) that said "The meaning of insanity is doing the same thing over and over expecting different results." I found this amusing at the time but now I can see where he was going with that statement. With that in mind, this brings us to the "Doomsday" theory. I asked myself is this "Doomsday" theory a plausible one and is this the idea I wanted to teach my children.

Now let's look at the "Doomsday" theory. (Doomsday Event, 2011) Many different cultures believe that one day we will all die because of the sin and behaviors of mankind. Well, this in its theory sounds to be a logical statement but in its implementation it is very psychotic. For one to achieve a state of mind where the outcome of that state of mind and their actions will end in total destruction of mankind is an insane state of mind, to say the least. I once read somewhere that, "What we surround ourselves with is what we become." So if everyone is thinking they will suffer some great destruction in the

"End of times" then their actions (because of their state of mind) will play out their destruction. Not because it was meant to be; but because they caused it to happen. This is referred to as causality. (Causality, 2011) So for the human race to cause their own destruction, when there were other alternatives that would create just the opposite, this could easily be referred to as insanity.

Point two and three are in governmental and religious entities. For these subjects, we will take a look at past, present and future. Through my research I found that all of these entities that were formed have three things in common. One, they have a "Head" or a "Top" person who controls or gives the impression of control. Two, they have a governing body which consist of a small group of people who are larger than the head but smaller then the last class which is the serving class or better, "Everybody else". (CIA Fact Book, 2011) So if we were to draw a simple design that would describe all the governments and religions, that design would be a pyramid. Top is the smallest then the middle a little bigger, and the bottom is the largest overall. But wait, it does not stop there. Every social class has the same design, and every economy has the same design. These designs could easily be referred to as a "Pyramid Scheme" with a different twist to it. (Pyramid Schemes, 2011) Sounds like to me, we keep trying the same design expecting different results but not achieving them because each and every one of these groups have fallen or been destroyed. The ones that have not fallen will someday because the design is doomed to fail before it ever gets started because history has proven this to be true. Therefore, my definition of insanity is, "When we learn that the design of something is not working and we keep practicing that same design with different players or in different ways with the expectation of it working for us, then this is insane." I am a technician and as such I know that if I have something that is not working because of poor design, then the only way that I am able to make it work properly is to change the design. Sure I can patch the old version up and paint it a different color. This will allow it to work for a little while but in the end it always breaks. To best put this, I would like to list some more quotes from my man Albert Einstein. These are a few, "We cannot solve our problems with the same thinking we used when we created them". Another one I like is, "Any intelligent fool can make things bigger and more complex... It takes a touch of genius - and a lot of courage to move in the opposite direction" and finally "Learn from yesterday, live for today, hope for tomorrow. The important thing is not to stop questioning".

So where does this lead us? Do we simply give up on our faith or our beliefs? No of course not, but we do redirect them to a scenario that is plausible instead of psychotic. What is plausible? Well, the American Indians, before they were corrupted, had a plausible plan in place that worked very well, Martin Luther King, Gaudi, Mohammed and even Jesus had a plausible design that would have worked very well if the designs were implemented without the restrictions of money, government, racial prejudice, borders, fear, superstition, politics, and many other restrictions, (or disqualifying factors) that by their shear design, are a hindrance instead of a asset. All these men fall under a category I would call visionaries or as some say prophets. (Visionary, 2011) Today there is another person who is an equal to these men of the past and he has a vision of sorts but his ideas are very reachable and attainable for all of mankind. We already have the resources necessary to make his vision come true, we already have the need to make his vision come true, and we already have the abilities to make his vision come true. Basically at present we are missing one thing and that one thing is our "Mind set". This man's name is Jacque Fresco and he, like a growing select few, would like to see our society become a "Resource Based" society. (The Venus Project, 2011) Right now, the whole world falls under a "Monetary Based" society where "Money" or "Wealth" is the controlling factor of all resources. In a "Resource Based" society, humanity is in control of all resources and share equality among those resources. Fresco also wants to put mankind back in "Harmony" with nature through the use of technology. His basic design is much like the design of the human cell that is within our bodies. One could also say the design is much like the universe itself. Each part of this society works together for the common good of the whole as every part shares equality in the experience. With this kind of design, mankind stands a better chance for survival and would move beyond the borders of our own solar system. We would be able to plant our seed on other worlds much like our own to take humanity to its next level of existence. This design is called "The Venus Project" and can be found in many means of media available to us. Fresco is also referenced by a group called "The Zeitgeist Movement" which is an organization that was developed through the efforts of a man named Peter Joseph. "The Zeitgeist Movement" supports "The Venus Project" but its main purpose is to help educate the people about a "Resource Based Society". They also support many other sources whose goal is a RBE. (Zeitgeist Movement, 2011) One such source is a project called "Cradle to Cradle". In this project they are rediscovering ways to help humans and nature co-exists where both exist in harmony and are fully sustainable. I am not sure why they named the fore mentioned groups, the names they did. It would be interesting to note that "Venus" in Roman Mythology means, "The goddess of love and beauty" and Zeitgeist means, "The spirit of the times" or "The spirit of the age". These movements are based on a whole new design but unlike our current design; their end result is the preservation of mankind, the planet earth, and the universe. With these designs, we would live in harmony not only with each other but with the stars as well.

When I first found out about these organizations, I decided to perform a test with the main areas that mankind is faced with today. These areas were religion, technology, science, politics, art, and economics. I asked various different people from different parts of the world to give me an objective view of two subjects and let me know what they found. In the areas of religion, politics, and economics I was told they would not work and they were utter nonsense. The religious Guru I asked actually shut me out of his life and broke off all means of communication with him. This surprised me because I was not asking anything but for him to give me his objective view of these two subjects: "What is the Zeitgeist Movement?" and "What is the Venus Project?" I also informed him I was doing this for research on a book that I was writing; which is the book your reading now. In the areas of technology, art, and science, I was told they were a very plausible idea but might be a hard sale. With me they were a hard sale as well but what finally got me to support these organizations was the end result. The end result of the monetary system simply was not that appealing to me. With a "Monetary Based" society, all the areas mentioned above are controlled by the use of money in some way or another. The "Monetary Based" societies all talk or promise of a day of great glory and great wealth with no pain, no wars, and so forth and so on. However, the vehicle in which they use to achieve this "Promise" is full of the things they say we will be free from with no plan in place to achieve oneness except an "I -owe-u" note from a fictitious "promise" that was thought up from fear and superstition. With a "Resource Based" society, there is no need for a promise because we are already achieving an oneness with the planet and humanity plus it will allow us to cultivate and excel in areas such as science, recreation, technology, health, and culture. Humanity would work as a collective where all mankind would benefit and have equality in every part of our world and its many resources. This in turn would eliminate war, hunger, pain, disease, homeless conditions, unnecessary deaths, crime, violence, and many other areas that impact us negatively today. Mankind would live in harmony with the planet as well which in turn would eliminate "Mother nature" killing thousands of humans on a regular basis. (Live Science, 2011)

Chapter IV

Our Faith

I have seen many things and interacted with many different religions, cults, organizations, gangs, and groups. I have belonged to groups like Amway, The Way, Church of Christ, Baptist, First Baptist, Second Baptist, Methodist, Catholic, Church of God, Friendship Baptist, Fellowship Baptist, Herbalife, Premier Team International, and so many others that I simply cannot remember them all. During this time, I have discovered many truths that seem to exist within each of these and other organizations out there. These truths are: (One) they all seem to believe that their system or way is the right way to perceive an idea and will lead you to true salvation of some sort. (Two) They all use a failed system of checks and balances to orchestrate and lead within their groups. (Three) They all believe in some sort of fictitious promise that usually surrounds fear, worry, pain, superstition, and many other areas that one would think to avoid. (Four) They all have togetherness that last as long as they achieve obedience within their group or the group's excitement remains at a high level. (Five) They all have a since of belonging to something with a legitimate dedication to their movement or group. These truths are true not only in America but all around the world because I have witnessed them in many countries of the world and in my own backyard.

Now let me explain my answers before you close yourselves off completely.   With number one, I have seen all these organizations basically say the same thing either they will claim "We believe in this and only this"

40

or they will say "This is the only true way" and there are many different versions as well. Basically, these groups since of loyalty are so strong that it leads them to believe that the only way a person will succeed in life is through their organization. I believe that this in itself is outrageous because if we can only achieve success through one group's beliefs then we are doomed to begin with. So what do we do with all these beliefs? Try setting them aside; it's the belief we have in our separatisms that causes us to be apart as humans. It is funny but so many people talk about their God or Organization and how important it is but don't practice many of the philosophies within their group as well as what the one true "God" is all about which is togetherness, This God did not create Baptist, fags, specs, jerks, Mexicans, Americans, Israelites, blacks, English, Buddhist, Chinese, Mormon, KKK, Jews, Muslims, Christians and all the other labels humans tend to stick on everything which whom they come into contact. He created "Humans" and we all fall under that title, plus we all have the right to what that title holds which is the right to live. Preserve mankind and work towards that, and you will be doing the will of "God".

In number two, I have seen all the organizations out there use the very same systems that have failed for centuries and centuries. Let's single out the Christians for an example. They, for the most part, agree in a God, a Holy Spirit, and a person named Jesus who is the son of God and came to earth to save this planet from its own shortcomings. Christians are broken up into many sects, none of which seem to agree with each other in most of their beliefs. They all feel like their method of doing things is the right way to do it and if you are not on board with that, then you are a sinner who will go to hell for your sins one day soon. If you take their Bibles and place the different ones together from one generation to the next you will find they read considerably different from one hundred years to the next and when rewritten in different translations. In some cases, information is taken out while in other cases it is added. The general ideas of Christian beliefs have gone from one extreme to the next as they try to keep up with the changing times. Most believe that their religion is the oldest and most prominent but in reality it's only a few thousand years old and there are many religions that are much older. If you take the attributes of the Ancient Egyptian religion and set them side by side to the Christian religion you will find they are almost exactly the same to include things such as the Ten Commandments and having a savior who was born of a virgin, died and arose on the third day and ascended to Heaven. Many of their beliefs are as wonderful as can be and very much to the truth but many are not as wonderful and far away from the truth.

They say it's a sin to kill but yet their God has killed millions in the name of the Lord. They say to have unconditional love yet they shun every group that does not believe as they do, there are many other areas such as these and you can visit http://www.evilbible.com for more information along the lines of this topic. They do have a lot of great practices but they hide many of their not so great practices and only the elite or upper levels have access to that information. The one thing that shocked me most was that almost all of their beliefs and ways were not of their own but mere hybrids of ancient religions that have long been forgotten. I was once what you would call a Christian and I once believed as they do but as my perceptions grew and the information grew within that perception I could no longer ignore facts and history that was recorded truth. Whereas the Bible was only a book that the believers of one man wrote 40 years after his death and there are no other known historical documents in existence that supports or backups any of the words written within, not to mention that many of the issues we know to be true today are not even addressed in the words of the Bible. I, of course, found these truths not only with the Bible and Christianity but with all religions out there as well. In every group out there, they use money as a means of support and politics as a means of control or leadership. These groups also practice having a leader, a governing body, and then all the other "servants" beneath them. Is this what God really wanted? I wonder indeed. I am still a firm believer in many of the Christian beliefs and feel they are of the truths that we all know in our hearts but they are not by themselves and in time the Christian faith like many before it will fail because it is not the song that the universe has been wanting us to hear instead it is only a part of that song.

Fictitious promises have been with us as long as

fairy tales have and as a fairy tale is of the imagination so are these promises. For instance, if your commit suicide for your faith, you will be held in great honor before your creator. Well that is a bit funny to say the least. Another is if you give God ten percent of all your money he will reward you with three times that much for doing so. Also, if we sin it does not matter because God does not care about that and you can sin as much as you want and you will still be forgiven. These are all very sad beliefs and it is sad that people resort to such things, God does not care about money or stuff and as much as we would like to humanize God this force has no part of that experience in our lives. Nor does this force care about prayers, it is our belief in those systems that give them the strength they have and nothing more. It is funny that about one percent of all prayers get answered while ninety nine percent do not, and people say it is God's will for all those failures. So you really believe that God wants us to fail ninety nine percent of the time? As a father myself I would never enjoy seeing my children fail ninety nine percent of the time and I can imagine God does not care for that either. But in that way of thinking, in most humans, is where the problem is.

Obedience within an organization is ok as long as it is a place of work, a military, or within a sports arena, but having obedience within a religious organization may be very dangerous. I hear people claim that our religions need obedience so that they survive and the body of this religion does as it is told. Well, you can describe the same philosophy with slavery, and neither one is any good and causes us to give up our right to humanity as well as ourselves. This does not mean I support lawlessness. It just means I don't support a mass psychosis thought that we have to give up our individuality to achieve an oneness within a group or organization. We should embrace that individuality instead of suppress or control it on a regular basis. Humans working together as a group while maintaining their individuality would be the supreme method within a group or organization with the best results.

Finally, it is important to have a since of belonging within any group or organization but to turn that belonging into a ritualistic way to control our thoughts and actions is where we terribly start to travel down the wrong road of life. Our since of belonging spans from something that is beyond our control but what we do with it is not. We must always remember one basic fact over all others when it comes to belonging and that fact is we are all HUMAN and that is something that will never change. Using our sense of belonging to separate ourselves from others is an act against the natural and a step towards the unnatural. This type of attitude can only have an end game of death and destruction. If an entire group took complete control of the earth, say like the Muslims, and had all other groups put to death, they themselves would all die because once they ran out of other groups they would turn on themselves and destroy each other. So yes, we should have our groups that bring us together as a people, but we need to focus that togetherness on the entire planet and quit separating ourselves with all these groups.

Chapter V

Truths

With all that being said, does this means we simply stop believing in ourselves and our faiths, after all they are not real. No, we keep our faith but we do redirect it in a direction that is more towards the truth of our existence rather than all the junk we have fed ourselves from one generation to the next. Within all of our governments, religions, cults, gangs, groups, and organizations are little hidden truths and these truths are the very thing we keep missing because we are too busy with ourselves. We have had the answers all along; we just kept applying the answers to the wrong questions. For the first time a small group of people within the world are just realizing the truth of our existence, but there are many parts of the message that are still being lost. To better explain this, I have come up with some simple truths about our existence and how they are in relation to everything else.

#1

WE ARE NOT SEPREME BEINGS

We have, as humans, labeled ourselves as supreme in the universe. We think we are the center of this universe and everything revolves around us. Well this is simply not true, we share our existence with many other beings and although we have not seen any of these beings, officially, we have generated enough evidence to suggest that in fact they do exist. These other beings have come to visit us, so at least in this galaxy they are supreme because we are not capable of visiting them.   We need to stop thinking of ourselves as supreme because that is a disqualifying factor that will lead to our destruction.

#2

GOD IS NOT HUMAN

As humans, we keep trying to humanize "God" and in some cases we have even had him to be born as a human and live as we do. This is all "hog-wash", the one true "God" is not of the flesh but is of pure energy. The vast universe or universes all were created by this pure energy and it is in everything that is anything. The trees and animals are more in tune to this energy than humans are but it is still there, none the less. This pure energy sings to us in a voice that only our inner energy (or spirit) can understand but our humanisms keeps

52

getting in the way of that song which causes us to believe in a totally different way. Every so often, some of us become more in tuned to this energy and we share our thoughts with others, these people are outlets for us to plug in to. Horus (c. 3000 BCE), Osiris (c. 3000 BCE), Attis of Phrygia (c. 1400 BCE), Krishna (c. 1400 BCE), Zoroaster/Zarathustra (c. 1000 BCE), Narayana (c. 1000 BCE), Odysseus (c. 800 BCE), Heracles (c. 800 BCE), Romulus (c. 770 BCE), Mithra (c. 600 BCE), Buddha (c. 563 BCE), Tammuz (c. 400 BCE), Adonis (c. 200 BCE), Dionysus (c. 186 BCE), Jesus (c. 1 BCE), Mohammed (570), Thomas Paine (1736) Gandhi (1869), Martin Luther King (1929) were only a few of many that were trying to deliver the true message, but humanism remained to be a disqualify factor during their legacy. These outlets were meant to help our understanding, but this was usually misunderstood by many. These people may have been followed, killed, corrupted, persecuted, put into mental institutions, abandoned, or even exiled. Their thoughts and words seemed special to some, while it made others angry. It has been this way since man has been able to understand and record information. Only today, with the help of the internet, is mankind able to share its thoughts and knowledge with thousands as they explore the world of the internet. I have been exploring this world for many years and have explored thousands of articles and videos from other nations which have increased my knowledge in ways that I never thought possible. This increase in knowledge has also increased my perceptions and changed many areas of the way I think as to the way that I am. To find the true God one only needs to strip themselves of all things in and about this world humans have created, then clear their minds of everything and just listen to the inner parts of themselves and engage with the energy that surrounds us all the time. The trees, rocks and other types of nature do this, the animals do this, and in most cases, babies do this. They are able to do this because they do not have any disqualifying factors that limit their abilities the way most adult humans do. Many believe our God to be a father, an object, a king, and many other human restrictions that are nothing more than our fears and superstitions becoming reality. The "Force", that is within us and everything else, is not concerned with our trivial human ways. It sees us the same way as it sees the planets, stars, black holes, and all the other amazing things within our many universes. All these things were originally designed to co-exist in harmony with one another but the balance is sometimes tampered with by beings who have reached a certain level of intelligent thought. These beings are allowed to explore this thought with the hopes they become aware of the balance of the universe and how it and its creator work in harmony as one. We have been handed down truths written within the many pages of many items such as the Bible, Koran, and many other books and readings. But only now are we able to find these hidden truths when we read from books of different religions, science and such, then look in the places where they are the same in thought and action. Those searching will find hidden truths in those places, but only if they are willing to accept the writings of people from around the world instead of just one small group or organization. Every part of mankind is a piece of a puzzle and when each piece is applied in its right order to the overall puzzle, in the end you will have the answers that so many seek today. Our "God" has given us these answers but until we seek the right choices of finding them out we will never truly know their content. If we chose to ignore the music that is within us and stay as we are, then destruction is our final end and the energy within us will be redistributed into the universe. The human race and the planet earth will be gone forever. The small titles and sayings, to include our writings, which have seemed to be the most grand, important and true, in reality they are of a limited source. The force that is within us is not limited to such things nor does it need our explanations and worship for it to continue to do the task it has been doing before the earth was ever formed. If we as humans want to get closer to the truth, then we simply eliminate "our human ways" from the equation and we will get closer to the truth of what lies within ourselves and everything that exists. The Zeitgeist Movement is a group that is in the infancy of understanding this as well as The Venus Project, but many within these organizations still cling to the old ways of humans and this hurts the organizations and the truth they are trying to reach. They are on the right track and one would hope they reach their goal but unfortunately humans have run out of the thing they call time. This book is an attempt by me to express all that I have seen and experienced so that everyone that reads within its pages understands what is at stake if they do not take action. We will lose what we hold so dear and that is our lives and our planet. If we decide to preserve these items then this force will take us to our next level of existence and so on; but this will not happen until we as a human race are ready for it.

#3

PLANET EARTH AND HUMANS ARE FINITE

Most humans think of themselves as something greater than what they really are. The fact is, if we take humans and line them up in a row then shoot each one of them, you will find they all die pretty much the same. If they are rich, poor, white, black, or the many other labels humans use, it won't make any difference as to how they die. Our planet is the same way. It has a limited source in which it operates, as do humans, and in time some of these sources will be gone while others remain until they are gone. Humans have figured out ways to synthesize new sources that are very similar to the original design but these come with a price which leads to much destruction and pain if used in the wrong ways. This synthesizing of elements is usually done with materials that are used to support us, but we do still rely on natural products from our planet to support our bodies and the health of that body. In addition, the air we breathe comes from trees which are only housed on this earth as far as we know. So for us to just simply keep using products and services and wasting the resources we have, is not very intelligent. We will destroy ourselves from our own selfish and self-sided ways. There is only one planet earth and there are only one species called humans. So if we want as remain to be part of the universe, than we had better put down our ridiculous human ways and learn to embrace the ways of the universe. The universe is all about preservation and respect as well as life. It allows all within it to have a sharing of knowledge and the elements, but this is written in our genetics and the very elements that make up this world as well as any others. We have the ability to become part of this song that the universe has been singing before the earth was ever formed. There is a saying, "The circus will soon leave town so you better catch that last show". We, as humans, have abused all that the force within us has given us and we have turned it into items that allow our greed, fears and superstitions to run wild while the truth lies hidden within our many fascists of life. We have the answers we seek; we are just seeking in the wrong places. We have been circling the desert for centuries, missing the promise land because we have let disqualifying factors control our destiny. We are not eternal and this planet is not eternal as well and if we wish to continue our journey, then we must come together as a whole and focus on two simple tasks; which are the preservation of mankind and the preservation of this planet.

#4

WE ARE ALL PART OF A GREATER FAMILY

Every since the beginning of time, we have been part of a family, of some sort, but our since of family comes from something far greater than ourselves. The universe and its many mysteries are in many ways, our first encounter with family. If you were to take us apart at the subatomic level, you would find that our bodies are made up of the same stuff that stars are made of. In a greater sense the universe and universes all are made of the same elements only the sequence of those elements are different in everything the elements exist in. I once heard it said that we are made from star stuff, a fact that is undeniable. So what am I trying to say? Well, the song we humans have within us is the same song that all life, as we know it and do not know it, has within it. Everything from us to trees, dirt, rocks, flowers, bugs, dogs, cats and all the other plants and animals here and throughout the universe have this same song within it. We are also all connected in a way that spans beyond our comprehension which is why mankind has abused so much since the existence of mankind. To put this in a simple term "We are all as one" and our creator gave us all a song that vibrates within our cells that if we are in tune with the planet and in harmony with the universe we will indeed here its song and the message within. Many have heard this message, to include myself, over the years but as such, most people do not believe what has been said or the people themselves misinterpreted the message or let the power and knowledge of such a message corrupt their thought process. Then the message is lost forever. Some have tried to write this message down, and for the most part they have gotten many parts of it right while there are several parts that are wrong. The one thing I have found that uncovers the true message is to take all that mankind has recorded from different religions, groups, gangs, cults, businesses, governments, churches, and all the other social groups we have, and instead of looking at where they differ, start looking at where they are the same or similar. When we do, the puzzle of life will start to reveal itself to us and we will be one step closer to the truth about us and our God as well as the family we belong to. The American Indians understood this before white man came and destroyed their way of life. They had as much respect for animals and plant life as they did their own. The Indians understood that we were part of a larger family and we must respect this family if we are to remain in harmony with it. Our planet has been patient with us for so many years and we have continued to destroy many parts of it with little regard to it or the other species that live on it. This is not the way our God wanted and in fact our God wanted us to protect this planet and treat it with respect as well as everything within and on the planet. Our planet and all that is within it, is just as much as our family as our own moms, dads, children and so forth. Our own universe is as much as our family as well and so on and so forth. We are all part of this family and we all have this song from the force that created the universe and all things within. We only need to develop this song so that we can once again become in harmony with the song that holds us together.

#5

Collect Our Values

We, as humans, have created a mountain of values over the years as we have grown in humanity and the world. These values come to us in four forms and these forms are able to interact with each other or survive separate from the others. This survivability may be long term or short term depending on the set of circumstances surrounding the values that were created. These forms are called (*True or Natural, Basic, Manufactured, and Synthesized*). I will make an attempt to explain each of these and how they interact with each other as well as how we can change our beliefs within each.

Types of values

True or Natural, Basic, Manufactured, and Synthesized

True or Natural and Basic Values

True or Natural and Basic values are values that we all share within each culture or race. We all have some basic value that we try to hold onto throughout our lives. These values change from one group or another but in reality, these values remain the same. Values such as feeding one's self, protection, self worth, are a few that have been with every society since man has been aware of its existence. In order for a person to survive, they would need to eat and drink water, provide themselves with some form of shelter, and procreate their species. If the human species has these basic values, one would think that humans could survive for an eternity. This would be true if it were not for all the disqualifying values we have made for ourselves. Although we produce many other items we call values, we do not need them for basic survival. Electricity is considered valuable but there are those on this planet that know nothing about electricity and this would not hold value to them unless someone taught them how electricity could be a value. This is where manufactured and synthesized values come into play.

Manufactured and Synthesized Values

Today there are tribes of people who know nothing about electricity, manufacturing, modernization, religions, clothing, style, cultural awareness, politics, money, and many other items that most seem to think have some sort of value. Yet, even though they know nothing of these things, their tribe remains to exist and grow within their part of the world. These people have what is called the "Basic" or "Natural" values or ways of life.

Then there are the rest of us. We have so many things we consider valuable. A police officer, for instance, considers his gun to be valuable because in his line of work, he needs this gun to protect and serve. A business man may consider manufacturing to be valuable in order for his life to run smoothly and continue his business. A Christian may hold their Bible valuable because it has the beliefs in their religion written within its pages. These things and the many other areas of different religions, laws, and cultures fall into the manufactured or synthesized values.

The severity of these values and how they are used is determined by how the person perceives them to be true. Say that I believe that all dogs are green because the first dog I saw was green. For years, I believed this to be true because I never saw any other dogs except this one that came by my house on October 31 every year when I was a child and it was always green. Then one day a white, brown, and black dog comes walking by my house and my whole world is turned upside down because I thought there were only green dogs. The truth would have been that my neighbor dressed their dog up for Halloween every year and painted it green, and also did this year after year so I always thought that dogs were green. Then one day, some dogs got loose from their yards and came by the house and this showed me that there were dogs of many colors. After asking the neighbor about the green dog, I find out there are no green dogs. This is how we put value on things, we see what it is, and then we take our own perceptions within us and put it into a category that either gives it value or devalues it. Then until something impacts us in a positive or negative way, we never change this value that we have placed on it. I could give example after examples of stuff some people think that are very valuable while others don't give it any value at all. This is simply because, that item has not impacted on their life the same way it has for the other person. Say that you have a drug addict whose beliefs are that drugs are very important. The drug addict will do anything it takes to get to their drugs because they hold true value on them. Whereas another person may think that drugs are wrong and will do everything in their power to stop drug use with others. Both people have a synthesized true value in this situation and their level of belief in this value is determined by their level of how true they feel their value is.

Now once we have this value we like to place it

into a social grouping of some sort which leads us to many more values to be explored. If someone comes to the United States as a foreigner, they might hear someone say, "That's the American way". Then you drive down south and hear, "That's the southern way" or you go to New York and hear "That's the New York way". All these things have some sort of synthetic value placed on them but none are necessarily true. You can use this same example in anything else you apply it to; the fact is that many of the things we as humans consider to be valuable are not as valuable as one would think. The only thing that gives them value is the importance we have placed on them.

Our Values Must Change

In order for us to survive as a human race we will have to shift our values and the importance we place on them. To do this we first need to recognize what is truly valuable. Here is a list of things that God has determined to be valuable for all life such as humans.

1. Basic food, meat, vegetables, fruits, herbs, and spices.

2. Water

3. Shelter

4. Procreation

5. Respect for humanity (Love)

6. Respect for the planet and everything within (Harmony)

7. Sharing of information

8. Knowledge

9. Technology

10. Travel

With these basic items, we can achieve what "God" wanted for us to achieve; we should shift all our resources into the development of these basic values. Why you ask? Well, for instance, food, of course is something humans cannot live without. No matter how you slice it, if you have no food you have no humanity. Same with water, without water humanity will surely die. Shelter, well, we can live without shelter for a short while but sooner or later Mother Nature will destroy you if you don't have adequate shelter. Procreation, well that speaks for itself. If you do not make more of yourselves then you cease to exist. Respect for humanity, if you keep killing each other off and having wars to see who is right or wrong, sooner or later, you will kill yourselves into extinction so having a respect for one another is a must for survival. Respect for the planet and everything within, simply put, if we destroy our trees, we destroy our air, no air and no humans. If we destroy our water, animals, and the many other blessings we have, then we destroy ourselves because we need these things for our survival. Respecting these things and using technology to help us preserve them, is the smartest and brightest thing for us to do but no one ever said humans were as bright and smart as they could be. Sharing of information, in doing this we soon realize that we are not as small or large as we once perceived ourselves to be. Everyone and everything has a purpose and a need to be heard and understood. We should embrace our differences and figure out ways we can use them to enhance our lives instead of separating ourselves into social groupings that have no chance of true survival, no matter how hard we try to believe in them. Knowledge, is an item that can be used for bad or good but it is important for survival because with it we are able to achieve a perception that we need all to survive. Even the simplest of people are aware of our need to survive. Once we learn to share this need and figure out how we can do this with all on this planet, we will be one step closer to our true destination as humans. Technology, this has been important to humans since humans were born onto this planet, we have gone from grafting simple tools to help us grow food and build shelters to putting mankind on the moon that circles our planet day after day. Although not all our technology has been used in the aid of humanity, it is there none the less. We should use this technology to aid in the survival of all humanity. We also will need this technology to move us from this world to others in our distant future. This is for our survival because this world will not sustain life forever. Sooner or later, this planet will stop supporting life as we know it and if we do not figure out a way to leave it and move to another then the human race will die with it. This is not a personal belief but a basic truth that no matter how much you try to dismiss it, we all know it to be true. Many have written about this in their religious beliefs and such, but we should not focus on our destruction but instead focus on our preservation. Travel, this has

75

always been important to us because on this planet it has allowed us to find and receive things that we need to increase our knowledge, food, shelter, water, and all the other values mentioned. Travel also allows us to see other cultures up front and may allow us to understand these cultures better, or may not depending on the level of ignorance or prejudice views we may have. It is also the only way we will survive as a human race because to survive we must expand ourselves beyond this world and to do so we must travel to the many other worlds that "God" has provided to us. We just have not "grown up" enough as humans to enjoy these worlds.

Chapter VI

Humanization

Every since mankind has been able to record history and record their religions, they have, over the centuries, "Humanized" their "gods". We have done this in many ways, of course, so let's explore these ways together:

#1

We shall give him a human face and body

Basically, we have given God many human faces and many different bodies, everything from Hercules to even Jesus. We have Buddha, Allah, Jesus, and so many different others amongst us in the world today that it is hard to keep up. We want to be "gods" so bad that we spend our whole lifetime idolizing ourselves. The problem with giving "God" a human body or face is that he is not, has not, or will ever be human. He is pure spirit or energy and only the occupants of this planet are considered human. God gave us the planet for us to use as humans while we are here but he never meant for us to get so caught up in our being human that we make "God" in our image every chance we get.   So let's stop humanizing God and start embracing God's true nature which is spirit.

#2

We shall give him our human sacrifices and worship

We are told from childhood to give ourselves and sacrifices unto the Lord, other cultures teach their children to give their lives in defense of their God, as well as groups and organizations telling their masses to give of themselves in order to show their obedience to their organization and/or leader. All of these are forms of worship and all of them have nothing to do with the one true God. In order to sacrifice something, you have to be willing to give up something, then you have to be willing to take whatever hardship that will bring; and if you have a family, they too must share in this experience.   Is this the information we really want to believe? I for one do not! Why? Because so many people, over the years, that have tried to talk about the truth, do it in such a way that gives obedience to men and not to God. God, being all spirit, could care less about all our human needs and sacrifices. God is everything and in everything is God, so we are really only pleasing ourselves when we do these things. We do what we do to glorify us not God. If we really want to glorify God, we would do what we do within the realm of God and not humans. God is pure spirit or energy; the same spirit that created us, this planet and everything within the many universes of the everlasting space. God is the energy that holds these things together and allows them to destroy themselves when they are no longer in balance and harmony with themselves, their planet, and the universe in which they exist.

#3

Do you believe in God or Man?

We may spend our whole lives believing in something that is of man instead of God. God did not create statues, medicine, science, religion, war, crime, money, economics, government, drugs, social grouping, hatred towards another, prejudice, bigotry, crosses, and so many other things that humans have discovered all on their own. No these things are not of GOD but of MAN. We are our own worst enemy and as such we work

towards our doom and not God. Many of mankind
today believes in a doomsday theory where we will all
be destroyed by the hand of God one day. Really? Well
first off, God does not have a hand and second God is
about creation and not destruction. We humans will do
the destroying and not God. We are the god of our
destruction and we will seal our fate one way or the
other. God gave us life, then intelligence, and we chose
to take that and come up with all these ridiculous things
until such time we destroy ourselves. But we may
choose to do the other as well. There are two sides to
everything and for every action there is a reaction.
Inside each of us is the SONG of God that gives us the
drive we need to repair and fix all that man has
destroyed. The universe itself is the model in which
God created for us to use as a blueprint in how we are to
conduct ourselves as humans. That same model lives
inside us called the human cell and it is the simplest

example of this model. The very things that give us life, also give us what we need to have to explore our true nature and our true purpose. So you can keep on believing MAN or you can believe God and hear the song that the true God has. Harmony and balance verses chaos and imbalance; you decide.

#4

Made in His Image

We hear people say this all the time and in many ways it is true but not in the way most believe it to be true. When we refer to "God's Image" most think of a body, soul, mind, and spirit. But the true God is not of these things but of spirit or energy only. The spirit of God is the force that encompasses everything and is in everything. It is everywhere and in everything all at the same time, in fact, time itself exist only with God and in God. But this God that I speak of is not human and was not made in our physical image nor were we made in a physical image of God. If we were to exist as a physical image of God we would exist as energy or a force on the outside as well as on the inside. We do have God's energy within us all and some of us have come to know this energy better than others and they have tried to share this with others. When this sharing takes place it is usually met with opposition in some parts and acceptance in others. In each of those ways it is misinterpreted to the point where perception is of no importance and of no value except the human value we place on it. God is all the things we can call him but God is none of these things as well, to truly place a word as to what God is that word would be "IS" and only is. We as humans are not in control of determining what God is, but the song that is within us all lets us know when the time is right and with that we are to do as we should to protect and preserve that which God has made which is us, this planet and all of the stars within the vast universe and the universes themselves. That is where our responsibilities lie and not in determining who God is.

#5

Destroy the Human and Preserve the God

Every time we let our humanism get in the way it has destroyed what God has created. This is completely opposite of why God designed the universes and all within those universes. These things were designed for the enjoyment of life, not the destruction of life as many would think. This life, spans from one side of the star spectrum to the other, and these lives are considered a celebration of what God is. For us to believe that one day God will destroy such life and to think this God would want to destroy such life is human at best. God is about creation not destruction so this God has nothing to do with that type of presence. When we separate ourselves from this God, we then seek destruction because the life that was once in us has now been silenced to the point where we no longer here the song of God. This turns us from beings of God to beings of ourselves. No matter if we were human or any other type of species that may exist; this separation keeps us from the true nature of our being and from celebrating the true nature of God. It is when we let our human ways get in the way of our true nature that we do as we command instead of doing what God meant for us which is the celebration of life. We should work towards completing this celebration of life by preserving our species, this planet and every world we are able to come into contact with once we realize our full potential. Once we realize the "Song of God" all of our human ways will not seem very important in the celebration of life.

Chapter VII

The Creator is the Creation

We have all heard people say that God is the creator of all the universe and universes. This God stands alone as the creator of the creations. Then there are those who believe that God must not exist because nothing outside of the known universe can exist by itself without the universe to support it. God as we have known "him" to be is not the God that truly exists. The known and unknown universe, and all that is within the known and unknown universe, is the God that we seek. This God is not only the creator but the created. Many people think of God as a human figure, like a king on a thrown or the master of the universe. God is not human and he is no master, this God is energy, the very energy that made you and me and everything we know to be true and do not know to be true. We have, over the years, made the one true God an idol and the king of the universe but in reality this God is not any of those things. This God is the glue that keeps everything together, and the spirit of why it is important that the universe lives and breathes. Our own bodies hold the clues we need to discover this, in our own human cells. Within our cells there are many things that work together to make the cell live and do its purpose but the nucleus is the center that holds it all together. Each part cannot function without the other but one part holds the blueprint that lets all parts work together. Our solar system is the same way, then our universe and so on. All these things, in one way or the other, work together in life, but hidden within each of these things is the code or song that makes it all possible. This song is God. God

87

is all knowing, all doing, all seeing, and in all places at all-times. This God is not an angel, a man, an alien, or any other creation that we can think of, but this God is all the creations that is, was, and will be created from here to as far as the stars go. Many people believe that they die and go to Heaven where they will see God the Father sitting on a thrown and next to him are Jesus and all the Angels in Heaven. As nice as this sounds it is not true, the place we go is the place in which we came from which is the energy that is the very universe or universes that we live within. Some of us hang out around those we loved for a while trying to help them in their lives to a place of understanding. This understanding has become so distorted that we have lost the message and have begun to stop hearing the song of the universe and all that is within it. I once watched a series of movies called "Star Wars" and believe it or not, this is the closest thing that man has been able to come up with that best describes what God really is and how things really are going to play out within our universe and all other universes. Yes, this planet may indeed get destroyed or humans destroyed within this planet. Dinosaurs once roamed these lands in great numbers and they too had become an infection upon this planet by destroying everything in their path. The universe recognized this and decided that they had to go. So they were destroyed and a super-human took their place, those humans also got to a level of destruction that could not be tolerated so they too were destroyed. Now the universe is considering destroying humans as we know them today, because they too have become an infection that is harmful to the planet that they live on and the universe they live within. If we do not do something to turn this around it will be by our own hand we destroy ourselves with, and nothing else. We will be the cause of our destruction and not God.

We will be our judgment day and not God. This is the

one and true gospel of the one and true God. We must

work in preserving our race and this planet to become

one with ourselves, this planet and the entire universe.

When we have achieved this we will take our kind to the

next level of existence and see things we never thought

possible and could have never imagined. We must

throw down our human's ways, our religions, our

control, our pleasures, and all so many other crippling

human "disqualifying factors" that we think are

important in our lives today. These actions, in the

grand scheme of things, have no meaning and never

will. We have within us the ability to change our faith,

and if we search deep down inside our souls we know,

and have always known, the true nature of God but we

have let our human ways cloud that which we have the

right to enjoy. Our people of control have created a

world of control mechanisms that keeps us in check and

keep them in power. Occasionally, we will have people with great intellect and promise come onto the stage and tell of a story about a song that is sung in the entire universe. They try to relate to us through the things we have already created within our human world and we usually end up destroying these people because they cannot be controlled by the forces of power that keep the human farms under their control. Yes, you are a farm animal to these forces of control and they do control all that is within this world. Who dies, who gets to be rich, who pays, who does not, who has stuff and who does not. We all like to believe we are in some sort of control but deep down inside you know this is not true because someone is always pushing the buttons or pulling the strings. It is time we earned our inheritance and become that which the one true God is about which is life. God is the celebration of life and all that is within; not the destruction of life. We were to take this celebration to the ends of this earth, then the ends of

our own solar system and beyond. Somehow along the

way we have lost the song of God in the hustle and

bustle of our human jail cell we call humanity. Search

yourselves, search beyond that which you believe and

hear this song once more, rise up all and proclaim the

celebration of life and start to preserve such life. If we

do this, then we will truly get to know God as God is and

share in the creations as well as in the creator.

Chapter VIII

We Build Our Idols

When we look at idols or gods we can break this down

into two categories, one would be "known" idols or gods

and the other "unknown" idols or gods.

Known idols or gods are those we have worshiped

throughout the ages that are known by most people,

such as *Jesus, Gandhi, King Tut, Admen raw, Buddha,*

Sri Ramakrishna, Holy Mother, Swami Vivekananda,

Guru Nanak, Judaism, Krishna, Mohammed, Rama, and

the list goes on and on. The point is over the years

mankind has come up with many different gods to worship

since the beginning of recordings. Many of these gods are

thousands of years old while others are only a few hundred

years old. One thing is for sure, we do like our gods.

Some cultures came up with gods to cover every day of the

week, events on the calendar, or seasons coming and going

from year to year, while other cultures decided to have one

god with a son or some sort of object that makes it real for

that culture. These gods are of many races, colors,

opinions, values, makes, honors, beliefs, and feelings as the

human race has grown from its first existence until now.

These gods have gone from a more barbaric type god to a

loving god depending on the culture and the beliefs of that

culture. As man has been born and died over the centuries,

so has the many gods that were once mighty and powerful

and now are nothing more than a history lesson. Many of

these gods were born of a virgin birth, many died and

raised to power once more, many performed miracles, and

many had followers who spread their truth around the

world. So to say we love our gods is an understatement.

But are these gods really the one true god or are they

mankind's attempt to "God Up" himself. Many of these gods are of an image that resembles man, while others are animals, and various other things and walks of life. All of these gods were and are thought of as "The One" but it is my belief that they are the entire one but they are not the one true God. If it has anything to do with mankind or humans then you can be assured that it is not of God. Humans tend to think of themselves as supreme in this universe but in reality we are only a drop in the bucket compared to the many other species and worlds that exists. If we were to destroy all of humanity and the planet earth, guess what, God would still be God and the Universe would still be the universe. It would have very little effect on the grand scheme of things if we never existed. So with that being said we need to understand the true God which basically "Is". There is no word to describe God other than "Is". You say is the air God? Yes. Is that tree God? Yes. Is Jesus God? Yes. Is a women God? Yes. Is a dog God?

Yes. Is a cat God? Yes, Yes, Yes, Yes, anyway, I think

you get the picture, it is all God, everything, everyone, past,

present, and future. God IS NOT restricted by our human

ways, nor does God need our obedience for God's survival.

There are two ways to describe God and that is "Love" and

"Harmony". When we as humans engage into these two

things we tend to understand and benefit from the "Hand of

God" when we are not engaged in these two things we tend

to benefit from the "Hand of Man". What does God need

from us, well, NOTHING. God designed and made the

vast universe and universes and life has formed on these

worlds in many shapes, sizes, species and such. God offers

the "Love" and "Harmony" of this creation to all of his

creations and those who decide to be in harmony with all

that God created, experience the true love of God and the

true nature of their existence. Those who decide not to live

in harmony do not get to experience all that God has to

offer. Then you might hear people say "Why did God

cause this to happen?" well they are referring to the wrong God. People will also say "God will come down here and destroy everything" again, wrong God. We humans have caused our fate and the only person we have to blame or praise is ourselves. God simply makes everything available to us and gave us clues as how to stay in harmony with what we have, as well as, put into our very DNA the ability to progress in a way that will take us beyond our tiny little human existence. What we do or did with these things is entirely up to us and God does not care one way or the other if we chose one way or the other because God does not measure in those types of terms. Many cultures have killed, murdered, maimed, destroyed, battled, loved, worshipped, procreated, slandered, honored, sacrificed, burned, torn, and many other things, over the years. All these were considered to be in the name of their "God" and to them they actually believe that one day they will be supreme over all the earth and their God will rule the world. Ok well now let's get back to reality. The truth is, God did create this beautiful world for us to live on and in time move on to other worlds but somehow we lost our way. We stopped hearing the song of God and started listening to the song of mankind. The American Indians heard these songs of God, as did the Aztecs, and many other tribes before "Progress" came in and destroyed it all. There are, still today, some tribes that hear these songs and sing to the true God as they live out their lives. They know nothing of our modern world and live in a time that is all but forgotten to most of us today. Many people, like Jesus, also heard this song and tried to explain it to mankind but before it could be explained properly these people died from one thing or the other because "Mankind" was not willing to hear the words as they were spoken during those times. We are supposed to be in perfect harmony with this song and when we are, we can truly start to understand our role with the one true God's world. How do we find this song? We stop and listen, listen to the song that is within us. This song is within everything and is heard by all. When you experience this song, as I have, it is the most awesome experience you will ever have. You will at that time know the trees, the birds, the planets, humans and many other things that we have on this beautiful planet of ours and all the many Universes. God did use people to write the Bible and many other documents over the centuries but these things were written by a humans so the message within was lost by humans so how can we tell what the truth is and what is not? Simple really, God made it so that where all of these writings are "alike", is where you will find your truth. God planted the truth into each one of us and when you put all the pieces of this really big puzzle together, you will find the true nature of man and our God.

Unknown Idols are those things we still let control our lives but do it in an un-knowing way. They too can be considered a "God" of sorts because our lives are controlled and centered on the existence of these unknown's. For instances, drugs; some people believe they will not survive without certain drugs in their system. They go through anything to get them and destroy anything to make it right for them. Same could be said with alcohol, food addictions, candy, and many other forms of addictions that have surfaced over the years. The biggest of these is "Money" or the acquisition of wealth. We as humans have let this one thing control every part of our lives. Money controls our religions, our education, our food, our travel, our work, and many other areas in the human world. We have sat back and let thousands upon thousands die because they had none of the thing we call money. The strange thing is that money is no more real then fairy tales. It only has value because we have decided to give it value. The food, religion, education, travel and many other things all would work and exists without "money". So if we wanted to feed the hungry, we could do it with no problem; or house the poor, no problem, build new roads, no problem. We have the resources to do these things and the knowhow, the one thing that holds us back or restricts us is money. We could do these things to better ourselves and help others, we could do them for the love of humanity, and we could do them because it is the right thing to do. We could develop technologies that allow us to have products and services absolutely free and will allow us to free up time to spend with culture and doing things that most only dream about. Whatever we decide to do we must stay in harmony with our universe and everything it interacts with. To tip the scales in any direction will cause, over time, utter destruction. Basically, when it comes to unknown idols, you can give yourself a little test. If you find yourself saying, "I can't live without that" or "I must have that or I will just die", well, you have an unknown idol and the first step to getting yourself back into harmony is to recognize the problem then correct the things you need to correct and get rid of the things you need to get rid of. Finally, stop building idols, alters, statues, buildings, and many other devices that are used for some kind of worship. God doesn't need these things because they represent what is good and needed for just humans and nowhere else. God has bigger fish to fry believe me.

Chapter IX

The Messenger

As I continued my research, I discovered that books like

the Bible, the Koran, and others were not as I had

originally thought. At first I believed that they had

plagiarized the works of ancient religions when they

wrote these books because many of the same things

that were found in ancient religions can be found in

these books as well. What I and so many others have

been doing through the years, is we have been focusing

on the messenger of these books and not the message.

The "Song of God" has allowed it to be clear to me that

there have been many messengers that have presented

this message throughout the ages. These messengers taught, guided, and trained members of their group and they wrote these lessons down to the best that they could remember. We have always focused on the messenger thinking he was the key or answer to the message but he is the same as we all are "sons and daughters of God". Jesus, Attis, Dionysus, Osiris, Mithra, Gandhi, Buddha, Mohammad, and the list goes on and on, are all messengers of the same message. The problem is, we have been putting our humanism into these books and focused mainly on the messenger which gave it a religious twist to satisfy our need for control. In doing this we have totally lost the message in all the craziness of our false teachings and human ways.

These people were only messengers of God's message, and that message has been the same message century after century. Unfortunately, we have focused on the messengers more than the message and created a

fictitious world around the messenger that has hidden

the great message written within it. This in turn has

caused an imbalance in the human race. We have been

out of harmony of our true nature for a really long time

but some of us have heard the message God has sent

and the song flows within our bodies. This same song

flows throughout the universe trying to put and keep all

within, in harmony with each other. Some have become

lost and have stopped hearing this song. I hear it every

day as it vibrates through my veins and feels my soul

with purity, love, and knowledge. We need to take our

focus off the messengers and put our focus on the

message. It does not matter if Buddha, Jesus,

Scientology, or any other messenger out there, gives us

the song of God. What matters is what we do with that

song. More than ever we need to come together as a

human race and realize that the beliefs that we have

held dear throughout the ages are all part of one song. This song has been song to us for centuries in the hopes we would bring ourselves into harmony with the almighty powerful God. This God is the air we breathe, the stars we see, and the planets we live on and may live on in the future.

Some people believe that the only way to God is through his son Jesus. Well God never had a son and has stated of this in these writings throughout the ages. Problem is we have misunderstood this message when it comes to Jesus and others like him. True Jesus was a head of his time in knowing the true nature of God, plus he like me and many others heard Gods song. There have been many to hear this song and then they shared their knowledge of what they heard. But even the Bible agrees with the fact that says, "WE ARE ALL SONS AND DAUGHTERS OF GOD" therefore we all have the abilities of Jesus and if we get as close to God as Jesus did, we to would be able to perform the miracles he performed. Jesus may more than likely go down in history as the man who was the closest to God than any other here on earth. Once we leave earth none of that really matters, we become that which we once were and that is pure energy, we will no longer have any human needs, we will exists in our new form, and we will not know each other as humans but will remember the time spent on this planet. God's message is what's important to us and that message is one of love, harmony, and friendship like none other we have ever experienced on earth. That message is the celebration of all life both in our know world and worlds of the unknown. Humans have to start to hear and listen to this message because our time here is getting shorter by the day. People often comment that God will send his wrath upon this earth to destroy it. Well I got news for you; we don't need God to do this because we will do this just fine on our own. We spend more time on small stuff that makes no difference what so ever if it happens or not. We have been conditioned to believe these little comforts we have in life are important and we have to waste time arguing and fighting over them. Mother and father to child, child to child, neighbor to neighbor, town to town, and country to country. All do this in some small or large way. We argue about our hair, or cloths, cell phones, needs, wants, and cars, you name it we are yelling back and forth about stuff we feel is important but the reality is, none of it is important. The one thing that is important that we have lost sight of is our race and this planet. There is only one human race and when this one is gone it will be gone forever. I personally believe God created a beautiful thing when he created humans, when they are in harmony with each other and are doing as they should be then they are very wonderful to be around but when they are not they are much less wonderful. Many humans have and do hear

this song that God sings to us and they are performing

in the manner God wants us to, but for this to work we

all have to do these things and do them sooner than

later.

What Gods wants is simple really; perfect harmony with

each other, our neighbor, our churches, our

communities, our countries, our nations, our planets,

and our universes. We can start here with our planet

and go from there. If we were to pull our resources

together and share them with no money involved on a

Global level we would eliminate hunger, war, sweat

shops, slaves, and all the other horrible acts humans

commit to each other on a daily basis. This is not my

thoughts but God's and those of you that have heard this

song know this to be true so we should band together as

humans and end our horrible acts and begin our

journey to a world we can all be proud of. A world of

harmony with each other, our planets, and the universes. People say this is impossible but if we change our attitudes it is very possible. Recently, I watch a movie called <u>Soul Surfer</u> and in this movie there was a girl who lost her arm to a shark attack. At first, she was frustrated about her situation then she fell into disbelief about ever surfing again, but when her attitude changed to believing in herself and what she could do, her life changed forever and she became an inspiration for many. Our attitude is the key to everything and when we get it in harmony with everything else we will succeed in all we do or want to do.

Chapter X

My Final Perceptions

We have many perceptions of our minds and we all feel

our perceptions are right and the way to go. If your

perception leads to a divided world, an endless sea of

destruction, and pain then most likely it is not the right

path. Our path is set and God sings the song to provide

us with the road map to guide us through the path that

has been laid for us. Jesus and all the other spiritual

leaders out there is the conduit to our true God's path,

they heard the song as God has been singing it since the

beginning of time. They also acted on their beliefs and

in doing so they were able to bring us great writings to

share to help us see as they did. We should embrace all and live in harmony with all on our planet and the universe within. We should take all the great writings of all the religious leaders throughout the many ages and combine them together and see where they are the same and there you will find the song of God. We don't need politics, money, banks, Wall Street, trading, economy's, and even our current law systems which are all flawed and not necessary. We can share our resources on a global basis and we can work, not for money, but to better ourselves as a human race and keep moving forward to a brighter future. Everyone should be able to enjoy Gods great earth and not just a few elite who control most of these planet's resources. We have to act now and do as we should and remember we are all human and none of us is any different than the other. We are all brothers and sisters because we came from the same two people from the beginning of the human race so we should pull together and become

one human family united in bringing the human race

together in harmony and taking it to the next level.

In this next section I decided to do a little "Compare and

Contrast" which I learned as a teacher.

There will be three categories that describe the amount

of the topic that there is in each different society groups

(resource and monetary)

Category 1: Unlimited - meaning it is in unlimited

abundance or there is no true means to control the

amount there is.

Category 2: Limited - meaning it is in a measurable

quantity or it is controllable in some form or fashion.

Category 3: None - means it does not exists what so ever or will not over time

I will also show how the two subjects are alike. There are numerous amounts of sub categories and these represent everything that impacts our lives today.

Areas of Impact	Resource Society	areas both share	Monetary Society	
War	none	no	unlimited	
hunger	none	no	unlimited	
violence	none	no	unlimited	
rape	none	no	unlimited	
sex offenders	none	no	unlimited	
religion	none	no	unlimited	
science	unlimited	no	limited	
food	unlimited	no	limited	
space exploration	unlimited	no	limited	
money	none	no	limited	
wealth	none	no	limited	
power	none	no	limited	
economics	none	no	limited	
power struggle	none	no	limited	
technology	unlimited	no	limited	
government	none	no	unlimited	
taxes	none	no	unlimited	
lawyers	none	no	unlimited	
laws	limited	no	unlimited	
recreation	unlimited	no	limited	
art	unlimited	no	limited	
spirituality	unlimited	no	limited	
culture	unlimited	no	limited	
crime	none	no	unlimited	
education	unlimited	no	limited	
resources	unlimited	no	limited	
mankind	unlimited	yes	unlimited	
transportation	unlimited	no	limited	
environment	unlimited	yes	unlimited	
oil	none	no	unlimited	
pollution	none	no	unlimited	
population growth	limited	no	unlimited	
abortion	none	no	unlimited	
sports	unlimited	no	limited	

As you can see the many areas that effect

humans today are eliminated in a resource base society.

Now you ask "Does this mean you don't believe in God"?

Well, no, that is not what I am saying at all. I believe

there is a force in the universe that holds all that is

within the universe together; much like the human cell

holds everything within it together. I also believe this

force is part of us and we are part of it. The song of this

force has been playing for us since our existence, only

we have misinterpreted the song that was being sung.

There are those who heard this song and they got the

right interpretation when they heard it, but then they

became larger than life, misunderstood, or silenced

because they seemed so special and we either put them

on a god level or destroyed them all together. This level

of "GOD hood "destroyed the song many were hearing

and they were mislead to their deaths or destruction.

116

We see this all the time when man reaches a level of fame and he lets that fame destroy the message he initially was trying to share with others. The only difference between them and everyone else was their level of perception. They had reached a higher level, and when they tried to share that with others it made them seem like a "Prophet" or a "God". These people were nothing more than a human who had reached a higher level of understanding, than most humans share, through their extraordinary growth of their perceptions. Jesus is often referred to as the "Son of God" and he himself said in his own words that he did not do the miracles that people said he performed, what he did say was that their "Faith" or "Perception" was in fact what cured them or made the "Miracle" to manifest itself. (The Bible, Mark chapter 11 verse 46-52) but there is one fact that has been over looked all these years and, through the amazing world of technology

117

today, we can no longer over look this. All information that these men assimilated was the basis of their perception at the time of their existence, and since the information that was to be assimilated at that time was primitive, limited, and prejudice then, so was the information that they taught. Therefore, in its final end these beliefs or information has no chance of survival because they were based off of inaccurate information. Today we have the ability to take all the information from around the world that we have collected since mankind has been recording it and compare it to what we have today. When we do this, a new level of "Mind Set" is achieved with the realization that we must totally change the design of our existence or we will end that existence, but not from some god on a thrown but from ourselves. Not to mention, our universe in time will get tired of us abusing the planet it gave us for growth and perceive us to be a "Germ" instead of a healthy "Cell" and eliminate us all together. If we are truly in one and as one with the universe then the time for us to be in harmony with our universe is now and we can achieve this through a society that supports a "Resource Base Society"

Because I have interacted with all of the social mediums we have today as a technician I have made several observations. In a technicians world we are not necessarily concerned about what is wrong and what is right but more so to "What works". We have our technical manuals that explain all the details and give us measurements, charts, listings, graphs and even procedures of how to repair. But when we are making those repairs these things aid in our understanding but our own "Mind set" is what allows us to make the final repair. When we make this repair not everything that is in the technical manual can explain our observations and a technician then has to rely on common sense to finish this repair. This common sense basically comes from all the experience we have with everything we do. Life experiences therefore, I believe are great teaching tools but these experiences can be controlled or limited. When they are controlled or limited then the person who is experiencing this control or limitation will only be able to communicate within the realm of that control. For instance, two mechanics come to work on an automobile. One of the mechanics has gone to all kinds of schools, worked in a target rich environment, and achieved his certifications in all areas of his field. The other worked on cars as a child, has no schooling, did not do much work on them as an adult but loves to tinker here and there. When the first one looks at the car he says, "This automobile will not start because the negative lead to the lead acid battery has oxidized to the point where the electrons, neutrons, and protons cannot pass though the cable to the starter and therefore not allowing the vehicle to start." The other guy says, "It won't crank, hey" The first guy diagnoses the vehicle quickly and efficiently and has the vehicle up and running within an hour and charges you for the cable and 1 hour of labor, where as the second guy takes several days to repair it and replaces several parts during that time that did not need replacing then charges you for all the extra time and parts and tells you that your car is on its last leg and you should consider replacing it. Both of these guys had something they could contribute but the difference is the level of suffering their contribution made on you. Both had the same goal in the beginning but their level of perception controlled their approach and this approach is what controlled the amount of suffering you had to go through and the time it took to go through it. This is the same difference between a monetary base society and a resource base society. Both initially have the same goal in mind but where as one causes much suffering and has no true plan in place to eliminate this suffering and remains out of harmony with the planet that supports all life on earth. The other society eliminates all suffering with a plan of building strength and support in areas such as culture, science, and technology and how to stay in perfect harmony with the earth and the universe as well. With this observation, for me the choice is simple. For me to hand over to my children a system that in its end will lead to destruction of all life as we know it seems a bit ridicules compared to handing them a system that preserves all life and allows us to grow in ways that is beyond the imagination.

Scenarios to make you think:

You and a friend are buddies in high school and enjoy each other's company during that time. You are from a high income home and your parents are able to provide everything for your needs and wants, but your friend is from a low income home and does not have his

needs met as well as you do. After high school you

decide to go to college and your friend stays at home.

During your time in college you learn much and you

travel from one country to the next experiencing life at

its fullest by visiting and studying all the different

cultures as your doing this you are telling your friend of

your adventures. Your friend who is now working some

meaningless job has decided to break off all

communication because he knows that there is no way

he will be able to do the things you're doing and

therefore sees no need to be friends anymore. Once

your journey is over you decide to return home and

when you get there you look up your friend. You

discover he has been dead for several years and died a

violent death while he was drinking in a bar. You feel

bad for your friend and move on with your life because

you realize there was nothing you could do and it is not

your fault but if you could have helped you would have. This is a scenario people live out every day in our world under the monetary system now let's look at this same scenario with the resource base system.

You and friend are buddies in High School and enjoy each other's company during that time. You both decide to go and study the different cultures of the world in person because seeing it on the internet is not the same. Since your resources and means of travel are not limited you spend years exploring this adventure and eventually return to your homes, get married and share your many experiences with your children and their children. Wow, what a difference it made when you make the resources unlimited for both people and take away the need for money.

Scenario 2: You and a friend join the USO and with the support of your local church, you collect money and food for the starving children in Africa. You receive word that a small group of children received a portion of your efforts but a band of repels has stolen the rest and are now is selling it to anyone who makes the highest bid on the goods and they are keeping the money to help support their repel activities. During the time it took you to learn this information over 30 thousand children died in the streets because they had no food, shelter, or water. This scenario just breaks my heart to no end.

Now let's looks at it from a resource society perspective. You and a friend are aware of the conditions in Africa so you coordinated with your local group activities advisor to send people, goods and resources to the children in Africa and within 6 months all the children have food, shelter, and water and thousands of lives are saved as a result. This would easily be obtainable in a resource society because your resources are unlimited to all those in need of them.

Scenario 3: You start a new job from an American company in a foreign country and you have to use a bus as the means of travel to your job site. The driver of this bus is a (TCN) (third country national) and has completed all training necessary to achieve his CDL license in order to drive the bus. Some of your co-workers get on the bus one day and start to call the driver names and start to mess with the controls on the heater because their cold, which gives everyone the impression that the driver does not know how to work the controls. Since everyone believes the driver does not understand English they call him all kinds of terrible remarks during the bus rides. The driver, who understands perfect English, continues to drive the bus with a smile because he knows the heater is broken and that he turned in a work order weeks ago but the company has no funding to make the repairs.

In a resource base society you travel to a foreign

country and meet up with a person, by chance, who is from Pakistan and both of you hit it off and decide to explore the city together. The day turns out to be educational and spiritual as well because you both shared your cultures with each other. This is a much better result!

The point I am trying to make is we can achieve our "New Jerusalem" like what's in the Bible but to do so we have to quit putting limits on everything we do and change to a resource base society. Currently, we attach labels on everything or everyone and these labels are nothing more than a limitation or a prejudice view of people, places or things. . Labels such as stupid, fag, Christian, Muslim, Buddhist, cracker, nigger, spec, Jew, rich, poor, homo, middle class, politician, and the list goes on and on. (Ethnic Slurs, 2011) These labels, in their design, are a hindrance to humanity and have no chance of being successful because they cancel each other out which we have seen by looking at our own history of mankind. These labels also cause religious wars, property wars, culture wars, and many other violent acts that our world encounters in today's society. With a resource base society these conflicts are eliminated and the labels are removed. This seems to be a step in the right direction to me and in a resource based society it can be a reality. If people have the things they need in life then they are least likely to steal or take from others what they need. And if they have their needs met then they are least likely to perform any act of violence and destruction because there is no need for it. Do away with money and you just eliminated the pursuit of greed, bribery, control and many other areas that people pursue today. Will there be some growing pains? Yes of course, but as long as we keep our eyes on the objective then we will reach our goal. The goal however does not lead us to destruction as our current goals do but to unlimited abilities and unconditional love.

What should our goals be? Well first the preservation of humanity, second the preservation of our planet, and third possible colonization of other worlds. With all our different beliefs and feelings, we have experienced separatism in everything we do. This group thinks they are the truth and the way while this other group thinks they are and all these groups are canceling each other out. So here is a thought, why don't we put aside all our differences and beliefs and unite to save our world and ourselves. I seriously wonder if my children and their children will have the same as we did. Our planet is DYING and if we do not wake up to that fact, we will be responsible for its destruction, then what's the use of even moving forward? Once it is gone that is it, the game is over, all the thing we thought were important are not because everything is gone. Another problem with most ways of thinking is we are still thinking in the ways they did when they thought the solar system circled around the earth or when they thought the earth was flat. People were threatened and killed or their families killed in order to keep any information or beliefs different than the current beliefs from getting out. Eventually it would get out and our lives would be changed forever. Today we have this belief that we are the center of the universe. We believe our Gods and this vast universe were put in place for us. But when we look at the universe from a technical view our perceptions become much different. Our universe spans billions upon billions of miles; in a since you could say it is endless. In the universe there are billions upon billions of planets that can support life such as ours. So here is the deal, many would want you to think that this one and powerful god that created all this stuff did it just for us but that technically cannot be true. I believe there is a force that joins us all together and this same force is in everything everywhere. It is the energy that makes us who we are and when we die we turn back into this energy with all the knowledge we obtained during our stay on this planet. I also believe that some of this energy, of the ones who have passed on, are right here with us helping and guiding (what they can) us along our journeys. There are those who have had near death experiences, and think they were seeing angels, but in fact they were seeing this energy manifest itself into whatever form it needed to reveal itself to that person. I believe certain people are born gifted and have the ability to see these things before anyone else and during their life time they tried or are trying to relay to all of us their visions, but because we are so primitive we would turn it into superstition, fear, miss-beliefs, and many other things except what it was meant to be which was a model for our lives. The problem with most of us is that we spend way too much time trying to figure out who and what is right or wrong. I say we set aside our petty differences and work on what will insure the survival of the human race. The other day I was watching a moth in my window and it was trying to get in the window to get closer to the light. No matter how hard it tried to go through the window, it was not able to. Finally after all it's trying it died. I thought to myself, humans are the same way they keep following a false path to obtain some false light or wealth with the illusion that it will make their life better and continue to do so. But time has shown us this does not work and will not work as long as we remain out of harmony. In the end the fact if we were Christian, Gay, Black, Catholic, Muslim, and all the other labels out there, will not make any difference at all and we will simply cease to exist. So to hold on to these labels and continue our greedy little lives as if nothing is wrong, would be a fatal

mistake that leads to our own destruction. I have heard

many arguments about this and many believe that

people would not work for free because there would not

be any goal to achieve. Well, we are all currently

working for free because the money we use is worthless

and has no true backing other than the endless amounts

of dept. As far as a goal to achieve, I believe our goals

will increase and we will finally be able to do the things

we always dreamed of. If I took my family to one state

every year, then one different country every year it

would take me over 200 years to complete that mission

so to say I would not have anything to do is ridiculous.

We would finally be able to thrive as a human race and

advance in areas of science and technology that would

take us beyond our own solar system to many other

worlds in which we could seed our race and truly live as

immortals. Others say we must follow an idol like a

cross or some fat man sitting down to find our true path but in reality these are forms of control that lead you down a path that is good for just that group or organization. If their choices lead to destruction than its pretty clear those would not be the right choices. I have heard the argument, "It is the word of God and we must follow his Word". Well I have always said that you either believe in all of His Word or you believe in none of it. In God's word, he points out that we have the ability to choose our path and that path is not predestined to the point where it is not changeable. Yes, the Bible explains destruction and death in the end of times, but what if this is a test as well to see if we truly were paying attention to all of God's word or only using the parts that meet our own little selfish needs at the time we were using them. Do you really believe that a God that is as big and vast as the universe or universes would want destruction amongst any of the created children ? Or maybe we came up with that on our own. Many who have heard the cries of the universe have tried to steer us in the right direction and we chose not to follow that direction because it does not seem right at the time or did not bring us our selfish little pleasures of control. Once man had to decide whether or not the world was flat or round, then whether or not the planets and sun revolved around the earth or the earth and many other planets revolved around the sun. We now have to decide whether or not we want to fight for our right to live or die as the human race. The choice is simple, destruction or unlimited possibilities, hummmm lets see which one would I pick?

Chapter XI

Our Next Steps

We as humans have continued to try a system of failure time and time again because of the perceptions and limited mind set we have placed on ourselves. If we are to survive as a race of beings then we must change our perspectives to the point where a metamorphosis takes place and causes us to realize that our current monetary, religious, governmental, environmental, political, and social systems are not working and the only system that has the highest probability of working and will not only save humanity, create equality, restore the environment, but will also allow humans to expand

136

their growth beyond all borders would be a Resource Base System.

We must remove our labels and borders and come together united in the common good of the human race. We must realize that God's song speaks through all that is, was, and will be and the only way to hear this song is by living in harmony with ourselves, this planet and the universe. We must start to build a society that will support itself in all that it does. We start by education, then implementation, and finally sustainability as the final goal. If destruction is the end result then we must steer away from such things that lead us to this path because it will not add value to the common good of all mankind. Our technologies should be designed for long term sustainably and aid us in all of our efforts, plus they should remain in harmony with this planet and beyond. An example of long term sustainability is my home. It was built in the early

1800's and is still as strong today as it was when it was first built. It has survived for nearly 200 years, through fires, storms, people, and wars. Homes that are only 10 or 20 years old are falling apart and being destroyed much faster. Why is this? Well, in the 1800's in America, building a home was a major undertaking that required a lot of resources. It was believed then that you designed the home to be able to withstand anything that would impact it during the life time of your home and family. So they used the hardest and best wood they could find, the best rocks they could find and constructed it in the best manor that was humanly possible at the time. Their beliefs is why there are still many buildings from that time still in existence today and as beautiful and strong as they were new. Whereas today we sell the bid to construct the home to the lowest bidder, then in an effort to save money they will use the cheapest materials, and cheapest labor, and in the end they will have a home that cosmetically looks great but structurally is a disaster waiting to happen. Yes, many will disagree with me in an effort to preserve their pride but we see the results of these structures everyday as Mother Nature destroys them one by one. Yet we have structures that are thousands of years old and are still standing today. Why? Because of the way they were designed and nothing more. We can design structures that will survive the test of time, or not, the choice is ours. We can design a society that will survive the test of time as well and again the choice is ours.

We must align ourselves with the same way of thinking as the universe does and that is the fact that everything that is done impacts this universal environment on some form of level. If we do these things in harmony with sustainable life then success is obtainable, but if we do them in disharmony with no sustainable life then destruction is the end result. This

139

is a rule that will remain with or without human intervention. We must remain in harmony with all we come into contact with in order to preserve our race for generations to come. Our current path is a path of destruction and in its end will lead to the end of the human race. If that is what you want, then just keep doing what you're doing and you will be doing your part to that end. If, however, you want to see the human race continue for endless amounts of generations then you must act in such a way to support that hypothesis. Separatism or fear is not the answer where as community; harmony and true "unconditional" love are the answer. Simply being a Christian, Buddhist, Islamic, and all the other religions out there is not enough either. These do have many ways about them that are good and help humanity but they still teach separatism and are out of harmony with the human race, the planet, and the universe as a whole. The message within these groups is in harmony where they are alike but where they differ will only bring destruction. Finally we must remember what brings us life here on this planet and respect that life as it is. We should meditate and look within ourselves and hear the song of all life as it flows through all that is, was and is to be. We should ask before we take, and only take that which is needed. We should give thanks and praise not to some king on a thrown but to life itself. We have a decision to make and we can change our perceptions in our mind or we can remain with the ones we currently have, either way one thing is clear, our existence is in our hands.

Chapter XII

The Darkness

We have caused much destruction here on this planet and with that destruction, whether we knew it or not, comes a terrible price to pay. There is a law that says, for every action there is a reaction. Our misuse of this planet and the things we have been given has created a reaction that will come in our very near future. Those of us who decide to hear the song of God and find this song within ourselves will not be affected by this reaction, but those who remain out of harmony with all, will be. This reaction will not be a punishment but a method the universe in which we live uses to bring our planet back into harmony with it and all the creatures on it. This dark time will be short lived and when it is finished humanity will once again be given a chance to live in harmony as it should. Those of us that accept this harmony will extend the human race beyond all borders and lines. Those of us that wish to remain out of harmony will end in destruction and death. When this dark time comes remain calm, look within you, and know peace, harmony and unconditional love. These things will protect you as a mother's womb protects her baby. Will our efforts today be enough to stop this appending reaction that has already been put into existence? Perhaps, but we should prepare ourselves for the worst in case it does not. We were never in control of anything as we have thought us to be. We were given the gift of "Life" and allowed to explore this life without any intervention from any other source but ourselves and our planet. How this intervention took place depended on how we and all our resources interacted with one another. If this is to be the end of the human race then we have only ourselves to blame. If we are to expand the human race beyond all borders then again we have ourselves to blame for that as well. We now have been given two paths to take, at end of one path is "destruction" and at the end of the other path is the expansion of "life" which shall you chose.

References

Now here is some great videos that help explain what I'm saying..........

The beginning

http://www.youtube.com/watch?v=8x4sVR67wCk

http://www.youtube.com/watch?v=57XDLAR-f6o

But this is what "Big Brother" will want and what our reaction should be......

http://www.youtube.com/watch?v=QkWS9PiXekE

http://www.youtube.com/watch?v=WLrrBs8JBQo

When they talk about us on TV...............

http://www.youtube.com/watch?v=MTN3s2iVKKI&feature=player_embedded

When the chips are down and everything seems hopeless........

http://www.youtube.com/watch?v=WO4tIrjBDkk

http://www.youtube.com/watch?v=STcDMoQ4KT0

http://www.youtube.com/watch?v=FWW4KogocfQ

What we tell our soldiers........

http://www.youtube.com/watch?v=Ds85Zko0cT0

When our families don't believe in us........

146

http://www.youtube.com/watch?v=_Z5OookwOoY

http://www.youtube.com/watch?v=GQlzz6jGCfI

When they call you God..........

http://www.youtube.com/watch?v=LqeC3BPYTmE

When we give up................

http://www.youtube.com/watch?v=PXvpDoGrRGU

When it's against all odds..............

http://www.youtube.com/watch?v=FYXjE92K9dw

When they try to buy you off...............

http://www.youtube.com/watch?v=dH4p9BQ3V9o

Who speaks for the earth.................

http://www.youtube.com/watch?v=x0FR3gEvXJs&feature=related

When they call you the Antichrist............

http://www.youtube.com/watch?v=g_eZjEwmn-Q&feature=fvsr

Beyond all borders................

http://www.youtube.com/watch?v=gWr369wdAZQ&feature=related

In conclusion...............

http://www.youtube.com/watch?v=aUdB8gCMcXI

http://www.youtube.com/watch?v=CjNxUguxwjU&NR

=1

The end

http://www.youtube.com/watch?v=jaaVs5W6T6s&NR

=1&feature=fvwp

http://www.youtube.com/watch?v=QRBak_2X3Do

This Book

http://www.youtube.com/watch?v=NvoRat-

Tl_Q&feature=share

Works Cited

Piaget." *English Made in Brazil.* Web. 27 Mar. 2011. <

http://www.sk.com.br/sk-piage.html. >

"Theories of Human Development." *The Great Courses.*

Web. 27 Mar. 2011.

    <

http://www.teach12.com/tgc/courses/course_detail.as

px?cid=197 >.

"Human Sense Organs - The Five Senses."

ScientificPsychic.com - Physical Fitness, Puzzles,

Personality Test, Educational Software. Web. 27

Mar. 2011.

     <

http://www.scientificpsychic.com/workbook/chapter2.

htm >.

Heath, Ian. "Glossary of States of Mind." *Discover Your*

Mind. 2003. Web. 27 Mar. 2011.

     < http://www.discover-your-mind.co.uk/9c -

glossary.htm >.

Canney, Susan. "Biological Feedback" *Negative*

Feedbacks, Positive Feedbacks, Implications

    For Science of Global Change, an Emerging Global

Perspective. 2011 Web.

    21Mar. 2011.

< a href=

http://www.libraryindex.com/pages/3193/Biological-
Feedback.html >

Opuntia</a>

"Positive Thinking Vs. Negative Thinking |
LIVESTRONG.COM." *LIVESTRONG.COM – Lose*

Weight & Get Fit with Diet, Nutrition & Fitness
Tools. Web. 27 Mar. 2011.

< http://www.livestrong.com/article/129520-
positive-thinking-vs.-negative-thinking/ >.

"Earth Is a Living Organism Which Humans Are Killing."
Unexplainable.Net- UFOS, Ghosts,

Paranormal, 2012 And More- Latest News. Web.
27 Mar. 2011.

<
http://www.unexplainable.net/artman/publish/article
 1226.shtml >.

Firehammer, Reginald. "Feelings Introduction to the

Nature of Emotions." *The Autonomist*. USA

   Big, The Autonomist & HP America, 01 Nov.

2004. Web. 26 Mar. 2011.

   <

http://usabig.com/autonomist/philosophy/feelings.ht

ml >.

"The Major World Religions." *Om Sakthi Spiritual*

Movement. Web. 27 Mar. 2011.

   < http://www.omsakthi.org/religions.html >.

Lord, John. "Ancient Religions." *Home*. Web. 27 Mar.

2011.

   < http://www.worldspirituality.org/ancient-

religions.html >.

Carpenter, Edward. "Solar Myths and Christian

Festivals." *Home*. Web. 27 Mar. 2011.

   < http://www.worldspirituality.org/solar-

myths.html >.

Carpenter, Edward. *Project Gutenberg*. Charles Keller,

2010. Ser. 1561. *Online Reader Project*

   Gutenberg. Project Gutenberg Literary Archive

Foundation, 26 Aug. 2008. Web. 26 Mar.

   2011.

<

http://www.gutenberg.org/catalog/world/readfile?fk_f

iles=1446150&pageno=1 >.

"Pagan Symbols Adopted by Christianity." *Welcome to*

Seiyaku. Web. 27 Mar. 2011.

< http://www.seiyaku.com/customs/pagan-

symbols.html >.

"Pagan and Christian Creeds - Chapter 3." *Index -*

Edwardcarpenter.net. Web. 27 Mar. 2011.

< http://www.edwardcarpenter.net/ecpcc3.htm

>.

"Albert Einstein Quotes." *Share Book Recommendations With Your Friends, Join Book Clubs,*

Answer Trivia. Web. 27 Mar. 2011.

<

http://www.goodreads.com/author/quotes/9810.Albert Einstein >.

"Doomsday Event." *Wikipedia, the Free Encyclopedia.* Web. 27 Mar. 2011.

<

http://en.wikipedia.org/wiki/Doomsday event >.

"Causality." *Wikipedia, the Free Encyclopedia.* Web. 27 Mar. 2011.

< http://en.wikipedia.org/wiki/Causality >.

"CIA - The World Fact book." *Welcome to the CIA Web*

Site — Central Intelligence

   Agency. Web. 27 Mar. 2011.

      <

https://www.cia.gov/library/publications/the-world-

factbook/ >.

"Pyramid Schemes." *U.S. Securities and Exchange*

Commission (Home Page). Web. 27 Mar.

   2011. <

http://www.sec.gov/answers/pyramid.htm >.

"Visionary." *Wikipedia, the Free Encyclopedia.* Web. 27

Mar. 2011.

< http://en.wikipedia.org/wiki/Visionary >.

The Venus Project. Web. 27 Mar. 2011. <

http://www.thevenusproject.com/ >.

The Zeitgeist Movement. Web. 27 Mar. 2011. <

http://www.thezeitgeistmovement.com/ >.

"A Disastrous Year: 2010 Death Toll Already

Abnormally High | Live Science." *Current News*

on Space, Animals, Technology, Health,

Environment, Culture and History | Live Science.

Web. 27 Mar. 2011. <

http://www.livescience.com/6212-disastrous-

year-2010-death-toll-abnormally-high.html >.

"List of Ethnic Slurs." *Wikipedia, the Free Encyclopedia.*

Web. 27 Mar. 2011.

<

http://en.wikipedia.org/wiki/List_of_ethnic_slurs >.

Additional references:

The Bible, The Koran, The Torah, and so on.

All hyperlinks World Wide Web http://www.bing.com

http://www2.fiu.edu/~pelaeznm/images/Resource/Sh

affer/Chp_2_Lg.doc

http://www.articlealley.com/article_1529088_51.html

http://en.wikipedia.org/wiki/Religion

http://dspace.vidyanidhi.org.in:8080/dspace/bitstream/2009/5624/2/JNU-2005-087-1.pdf

http://www.historyguy.com/nations/government_types.html

http://www.youtube.com/watch?v=8x4sVR67wCk

http://www.youtube.com/watch?v=57XDLAR-f6o

http://www.youtube.com/watch?v=QkWS9PiXekE

http://www.youtube.com/watch?v=WLrrBs8JBQo

http://www.youtube.com/watch?v=MTN3s2iVKKI&feature=player_embedded

http://www.youtube.com/watch?v=WO4tIrjBDkk

http://www.youtube.com/watch?v=STcDMoQ4KT0

http://www.youtube.com/watch?v=FWW4KogocfQ

http://www.youtube.com/watch?v=Ds85Zko0cT0

http://www.youtube.com/watch?v=_Z5OookwOoY

http://www.youtube.com/watch?v=GQlzz6jGCfI

http://www.youtube.com/watch?v=LqeC3BPYTmE

http://www.youtube.com/watch?v=PXvpDoGrRGU

http://www.youtube.com/watch?v=FYXjE92K9dw

http://www.youtube.com/watch?v=dH4p9BQ3V9o

http://www.youtube.com/watch?v=x0FR3gEvXJs&feature=related

http://www.youtube.com/watch?v=g_eZjEwmn-Q&feature=fvsr

http://www.youtube.com/watch?v=gWr369wdAZQ&feature=related

http://www.youtube.com/watch?v=aUdB8gCMcXI

http://www.youtube.com/watch?v=CjNxUguxwjU&NR=1

http://www.dailymotion.com/video/x3zgc3_was-jesus-a-sun-god-part-3-wrong_people

http://www.facebook.com/l.php?u=http%3A%2F%2Fwww.dailymotion.com%2Fvideo%2Fx3zg1e_was-jesus-a-sun-god-part-2-wrong_people&h=485d6

http://www.dailymotion.com/video/x3zfs1_was-jesus-a-sun-god-part-1-wrong_people

http://www.youtube.com/watch?v=4Z9WVZddH9w&playnext=1&list=PL72AE25003C1DBA70

http://www.youtube.com/watch?v=EewGMBOB4Gg&feature=related

http://www.youtube.com/watch?v=YxPPnCW6sMo&feature=related

http://www.youtube.com/watch?v=cAjFBsp_aE&feature=related

http://www.youtube.com/watch?v=yCJqP18gBlc&NR=1

http://www.youtube.com/watch?v=tdhklzlF3Dw&feature=related

http://www.youtube.com/watch?v=Q1a5MlHFJu4&NR=1

http://www.youtube.com/watch?v=cn67i24MstA&feature=player_embedded

And the list goes on and on...........

AUTHORITIES. (taken from various sources)

Rawlinson's Egypt and Babylon; History of Babylonia,

by A.H. Sayce; Smith's Dictionary of the Bible;

Rawlinson's Herodotus; George Smith's History of

Babylonia; Lenormant's Manuel d'Histoire Ancienne;

Layard's Nineveh and Babylon; Journal of Royal Asiatic

Society; Heeren's Asiatic Nations; Dr. Pusey's Lectures

on Daniel; Birch's Egypt from the Earliest Times;

Brugsch's History of Egypt; Records of the Past;

Rawlinson's History of Ancient Egypt; Wilkinson's

Ancient Egyptians; Sayce's Ancient Empires of the East;

Rawlinson's Religions of the Ancient World; James

Freeman Clarke's Ten Great Religions; Religion of

Ancient Egypt, by P. Le Page Renouf; Moffat's

Comparative History of Religions; Bunsen's Egypt's

Place in History; Persia, from the Earliest Period, by W.

S. W. Vaux; Johnson's Oriental Religions; Haug's Essays;

Spiegel's Avesta.

The above are the more prominent authorities; but the

number of books on ancient religions is very large.

Copyright Page

Applied for copyright case # 1-709844701

US Copyright Office

Edition 2